TRANSPARENT

ARCHITECTURE

TRANSPARENT ARCHITECTURE

GORDON GILBERT

WITH ESSAYS BY MICHAEL SORKIN, ZVI HECKER
LEBBEUS WOODS, AND CHRISTIAN W. THOMSEN

TRANSPARENT ARCHITECTURE

Exploring the idea of transparency in architecture, this compilation of work ranges from open space and physical transparency, to clarity of structure, to the dematerialization of the actual physical object, and further, to evolving and expanding states of architectural awareness. This exploration is facilitated through a revealing juxtaposition of experimental drawing, subliminal texts, and actual constructed work.

The projects in *Transparent Architecture* began with conceptual drawing that was published and exhibited internationally. Then the seminal ideas and approaches earlier developed in this experimental phase came to fruition years later in actual constructed work.   Even across time, a consistent architectural stance emerges, and seems to permeate all the work.

First used in the 15th century, the word transparent has origins in the Medieval Latin – *transparere*, meaning to show through. It's original Latin derivation is *trans + parere*, meaning to show oneself.

The work in this book points to an architecture that appears to suggest a multiplicity of qualities. Paradoxically, it is also an architecture that reveals itself and its own singular nature clearly.

The structures themselves display their own material and organizational logic, yet they are also able to function as containers for thought, moods, and memories. The inhabitant then moves through and interacts in a live and changing world.

Activities happen all at once, in a seamless whole, in a simultaneity of experience. This is an architecture of natural processes in the revealed landscape, entropic and vital, where the normal boundaries and usual edges do not hold.

The experimental drawings, texts, and built projects on the following pages are visual and spatial explorations. They aim toward architecture that provokes thought, refines one's abilities to see, and embraces the ongoing confluence and mutability of things.

Architecture that reveals and reveals itself.

Roofs and walls step up and fold upon themselves like an ancient Siamese temple or floating Chinese junk. The space inside juts upward as a church nave or a ships hull, lifting toward the prow.

Architecture can be seen as ascendant, and trans-dimensional, subsuming time, materiality and space. It can be an architecture of knowledge, inclusive and nested through all realities.

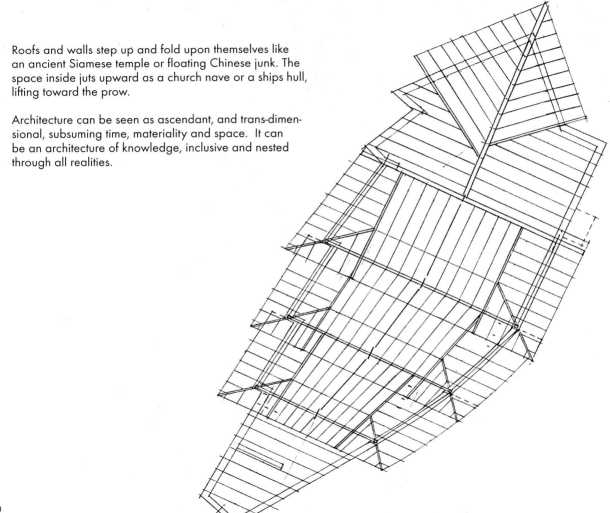

Into a forgotten world, instantly familiar, suddenly remembered, open passage within. With a certain movement, an old sense arises, with a shape and feeling long since occurred.

Hidden in a tropical jungle, these structures are usually seen only in fragments, their exterior forms seeming to intervene and grow from the exotic foliage.

As an oasis, this is a place of balance, calmness and refuge for individuals in a rapid and seemingly chaotic world.

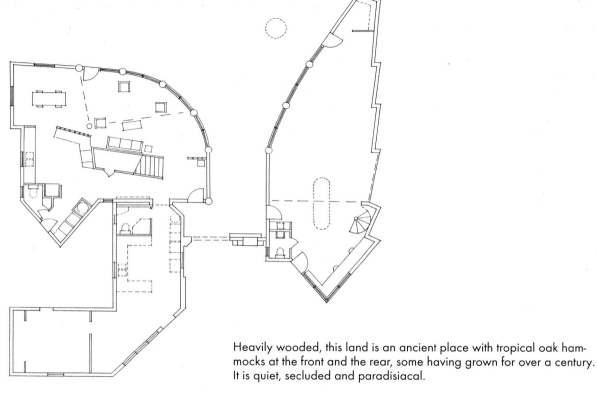

Heavily wooded, this land is an ancient place with tropical oak hammocks at the front and the rear, some having grown for over a century. It is quiet, secluded and paradisiacal.

This site is reconfigured and regenerated from within the branches and canopies of the existing trees. The forms developed are peculiar to this site, creating an architecture of this particular landscape.

Different from our usual experience, here is an exotic place, mysterious, in a twilight realm, subliminal and dreamlike. A place that transcends functional planning and literal thought.

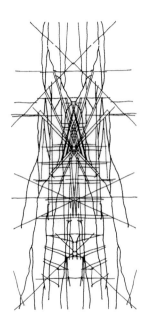

Foliated, twisting and lifted, the spaces have a visceral quality, resonating within oneself, and seeming to rise out of ones own awareness and the landscape simultaneously. The main interior spaces are central and centering, allowing the inhabitant to always feel as if at the focus of the structure's own unfolding.

The spaces inspire, as they move outward and upward, literally raising up and expanding one's sensations and sight. There is quite a bit of movement within these structures, yet the feeling inside remains centered, calm, and uplifting. These spaces and forms defer to the inhabitant, which will allow her to flourish.

Structural systems typical to the tropics and resistant to hurricanes are used. Spread and isolated concrete foundations support reinforced masonry construction, with grade beams in the rear to protect the oak tree roots. Roofs and floors are shaped wood framing supported and tied to girder trusses that step up the masonry walls.

Sometimes you are inside the space, yet it feels like it is exterior space. Other times you are inside the space, and it feels like the space is inside you.

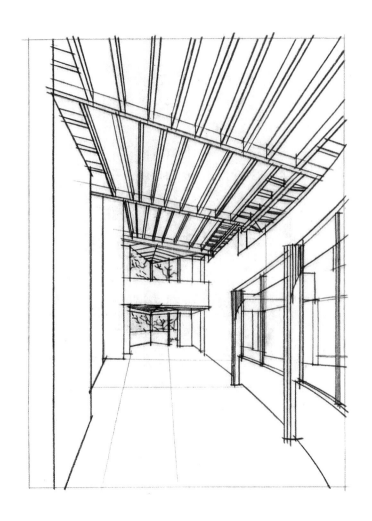

as the continually ascending and unfolding qualities in the central space of the closely held night sky

curved and shifting backward view

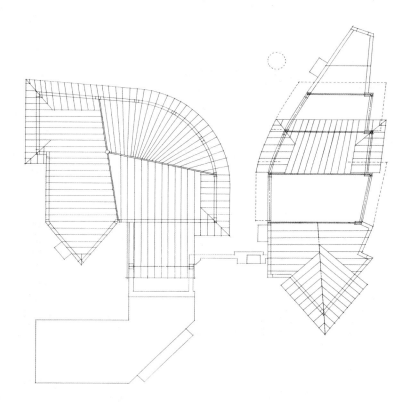

In this direction, the structure steps down in forced perspective to a single point, exploding forward, roofs and walls separating and lifting, seeming to disassemble themselves.

The inside opens out to include the exterior, while qualities of light and space from the land are extended into the structure.

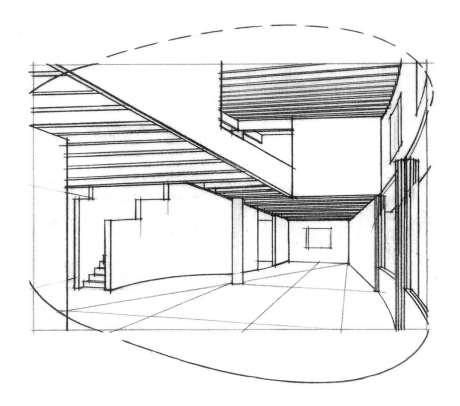

The adjacent structure circles, bends and fans around a central post, in a twisting conch-like shape. Its space unfolds, spirals and lifts. This architecture is alive and affects one positively. Light filters in and resonates with the outer light of the hammock foliage.

Luminous and personal, the boundaries of awareness and physical manifestation induce us to follow.

The two buildings split and pivot away from the existing fireplace, creating an opening from front to back. This split provides a trail linking oak hammocks on the site, allowing the inhabitant to see for the first time across the land. The ancient oak in the rear now becomes the central focus.

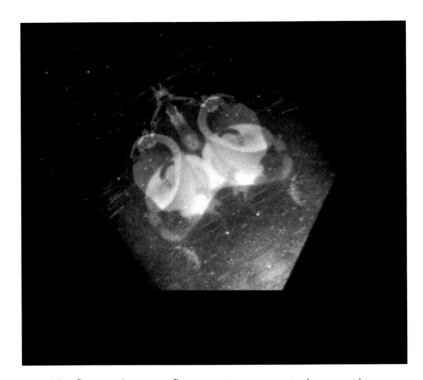

Within floating, hovering, flying, soaring scenes, in dreams within dreams, there is a shift from far to near, immediate.

Slip on thin garments of identity, played for another's benefit.

When the center is alive from head to toe then attention permeates throughout, and all endeavors go well.

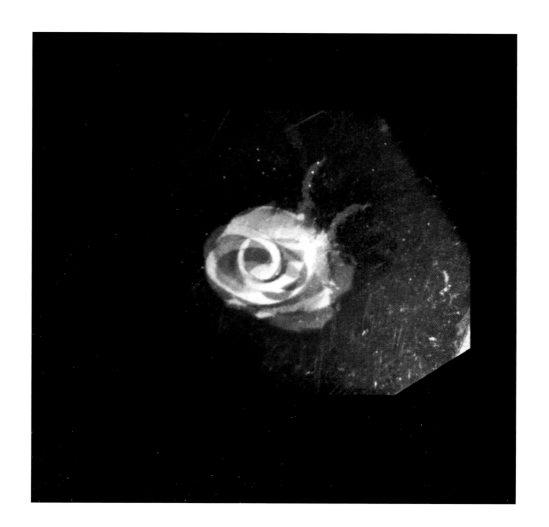

The body is slight, insubstantial, and air comes through the widening cracks. That which holds concepts together begins to dissolve, and physicality is diminished.

Then awareness floats free and hovers, and the world becomes as awareness itself.

In a momentary crystallization of the ephemeral, there is a shift from the numinous to the phenomenal.

illusory, paradoxical and steadfast

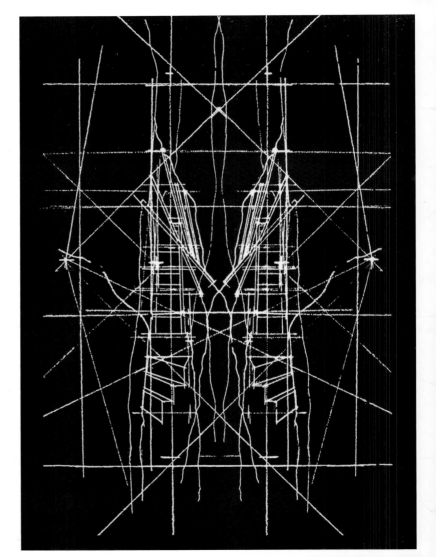

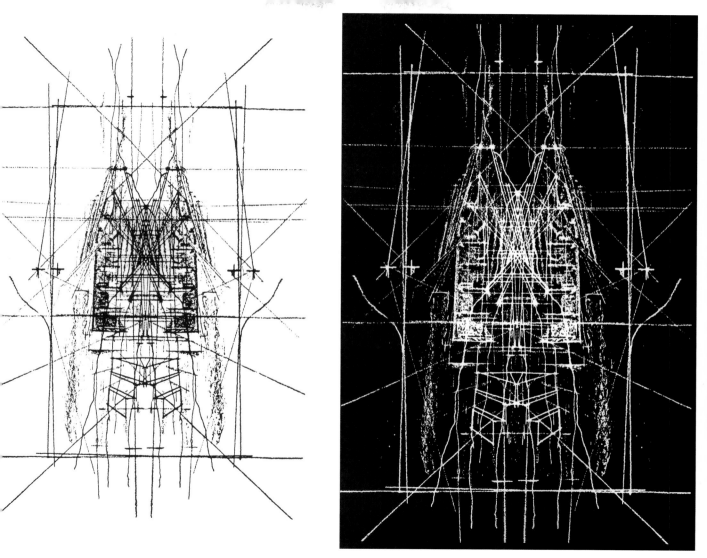

interior view of the leading edge

This land is in a tropical hammock in a high velocity hurricane zone, filled with the wild and dazzling foliage traditionally associated with this specific area. The structure grows from these natural qualities of the tropical site in its form, construction, interior, scheme and surface texture.

As a result, the structure provides a protective containment, yet at the same time there is an inner fluidity, where the spaces are not so obviously delineated, and the rooms are floating.

Turned protectively within, this structure is small, yet the strategic placement of window openings allows views outward to the thick tropical foliage.

Layering the internal forms without many doors gives an openness to the space, both horizontally and vertically. Thus the occupants become aware of the totality of the interior surroundings all at once.

The interior tends to reveal its presence gradually in the morning, as light glances off the smooth surfaces creating a glow throughout the entire house.

An outward visual focus can bring attention back to the building's source, its vertical central space.

All construction systems are hurricane resistant, including spread and isolated concrete foundations supporting reinforced masonry walls at both levels with flat truss floor and roof framing systems. Framing is anchored to the masonry at all points with metal hurricane anchors and straps.

Walls on the first and second floors have been strengthened and tied vertically to the floor and roof framing for additional stability and uplift resistance. All masonry openings have hurricane-proof windows and doors, eliminating the need for shutters.

There can be a direct connection, a corporeal resemblance. Notions of time and space can expand, not in some future world, but nearby and already here.

Centered energy in visual form has its body analogies and inner currents.

Occurrences are simultaneous and in many realms, synchronous and contiguous.

Look out, look back, the street is thin, grayed, a thin veil, insubstantial, a mere excuse, quite different than what we had thought.

concepts flop, the mind flutters

Overlapping and echoing, phrases shift to geometric patterns, and all considerations are rearranged.

The house fans, folds and shifts, causing shifting viewpoints of the singular appearance, with the outside view ever present. It becomes a canopy and a vantage point from which nature reveals itself.

Structurally, the frame is an open reed-like bridging of hybrid members hidden within the glass window frames that create the effect of a canopied roof that seems to float with no appreciable support.

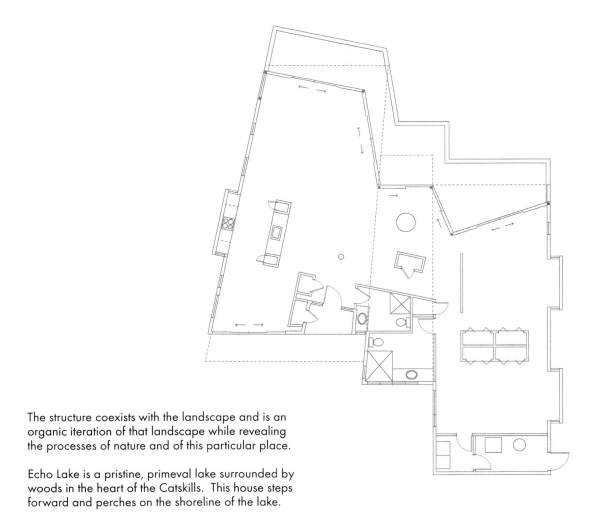

The structure coexists with the landscape and is an organic iteration of that landscape while revealing the processes of nature and of this particular place.

Echo Lake is a pristine, primeval lake surrounded by woods in the heart of the Catskills. This house steps forward and perches on the shoreline of the lake.

Opening outward and upward, the space inspire,
literally raising up and expanding one's own
sensation and sight.

multi-stoned, yet darkened, ruby-like, dusty,
gleaming jewel, a glistening form of the inner
landscape

It is a permutation upon itself, always present,
pulsating and ambiguous.

These spaces are opened out, allowing senses to expand, as the interior and exterior merge. Things can be perceived all at once, and the inhabitant is both here and there, in a live and changing world.

Materials are stained wood, stone and light, tree branches, shadow patterns, water and foliage, metal and ice, and the like. These change, waver, grow and decay, by night and day, through storms and sun, in all times and seasons.

Clear light flashes through the room dissolving the platforms on which the room itself is based.

The contents of the panoramic landscape allow themselves to be seen directly with all their subtle movements and changes. Light springs from nowhere and disappears again as quickly. It is an architecture that reveals, while also revealing itself.

Visual scenes arrive directly and without effort. The scenes are alive and congruent with our own selves. Sentient images float by and reconcile.

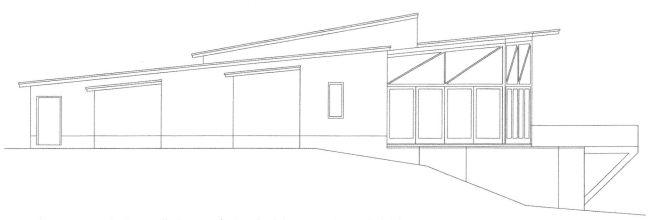

Window-wall elements facing the lake are set into a hybrid trussed structural frame that supports the roof and its heavy snow load, while at the same time maintaining maximum openness and resistance to high winds.

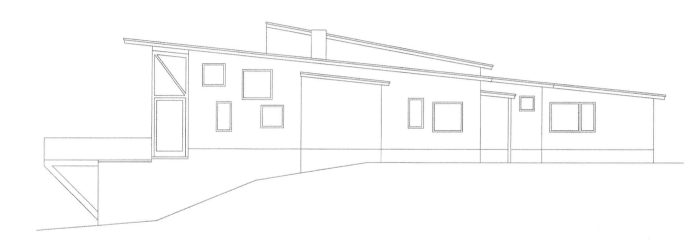

The wooden trunks and branches of the house parallel the structure of the forest, and the space within the house parallels the space without.

In these canopied spaces, everything is present all at once, including things reflected or transparent, or things barely perceived.

This structure can act as a land bridge, or a ledge outcropping, as a snow bank, or an open pagoda, a screened porch or a hidden igloo, all depending on the changing climatic conditions.

Shapes lose definition to become containers of light, where the outside and inside tend to merge.

This is an architecture of natural processes in the landscape, entropic and vital, that plays with the dissolving boundaries of form and space.

In an ongoing play of shadow and light, the structure mediates and the light reveals.

Things are tenuous, barely holding together, dissipating easily, and the world becomes as awareness itself.

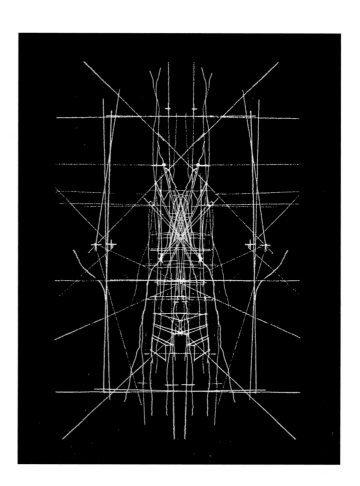

These open interiors can become light filters, windbreaks, rain shields or ice shelters, sunset panoramas, or visual screens upon which the varied qualities of nature play out.

Night, which is unconcealed and unbound, begins to spread out from the inner reality to invade the entire structure of finiteness. Novel and mysterious qualities are brought to life.

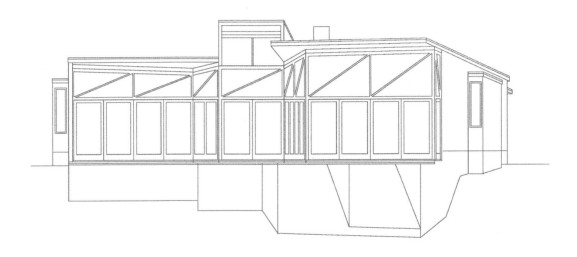

Use and function are simplified. Interior forms are arranged in a spatial flux and not separated. They are defined and used according to the inhabitants' predisposition, in a seamless whole.

Within the shimmers and shifts, inner focusing and paradoxical changes, there can be a resemblance; a direct connection, tacit knowing, unspoken, and a complete bond in a field of identification.

Things can be found in their entirety and all at once, rather than bit by bit.

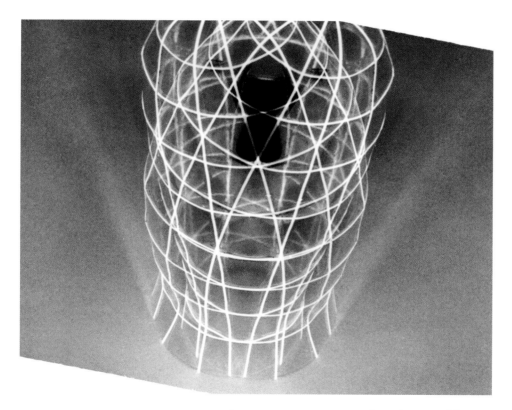

continuous cross-connection and simultaneity of form

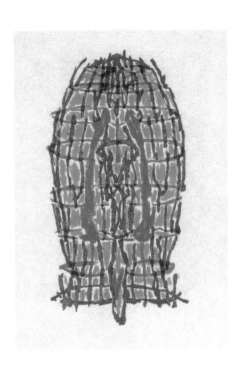

within centered energy in visual form with
their body analogies and inner currents

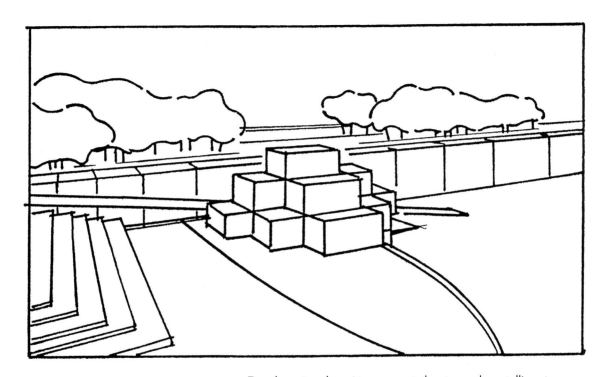

Translucent and semi-transparent, the stepped crystalline structure completes itself visually in the reflecting pool. Its wholeness
is comprised of actual and reflected imagery, and the form is
completed in the viewers own mind.

Thus the seeming solidity of the structure is in great part illusory.

A series of stepped rigid steel frames rise up off a base wall from all directions to a compression frame at the top. All the enclosing planes are structural glass.

These cascading frames seem to break apart and come together at the same time, as if in a state of creation and dissolution simultaneously.

and the discursive dissolves up into the night

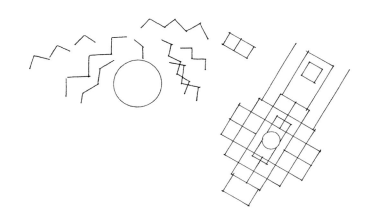

Changes in opacity, clarity, and sense of form depend on the time of day, strength of light, and the viewpoint of the participant. Thus the structure seems to be perpetually in flux.

As all this memorializes death, itself ambiguous, it is fitting that the structure would invite participation into it's own ambiguity.

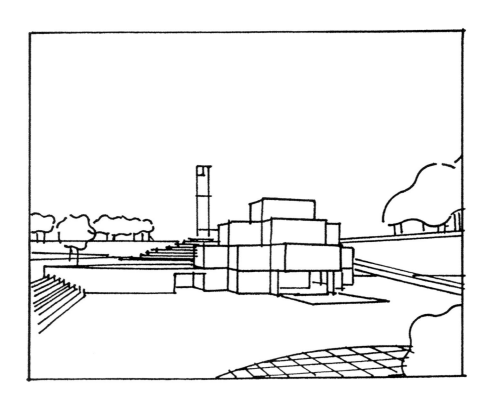

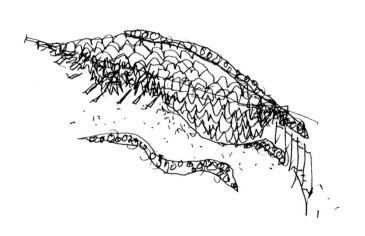

a mapping of forms, with their passages,
progressions and perceptual mutability

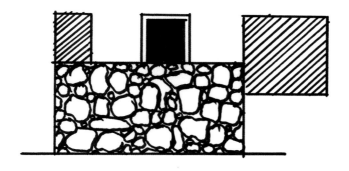

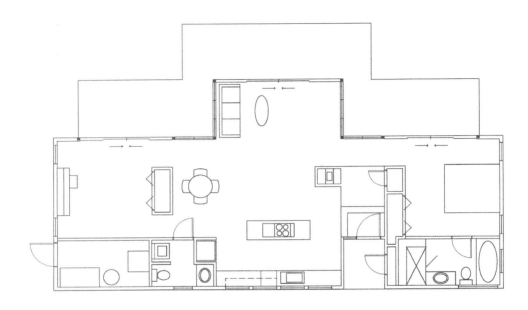

The roof steps up and down again, bridging the land and vegetation on either side, while visually merging with the shimmering waters of the lake.

As a remote parkland, this site has the feel of a secluded bird sanctuary. The structure is placed on a promontory of the sloping landscape so that its profile barely rises above the grassy plain.

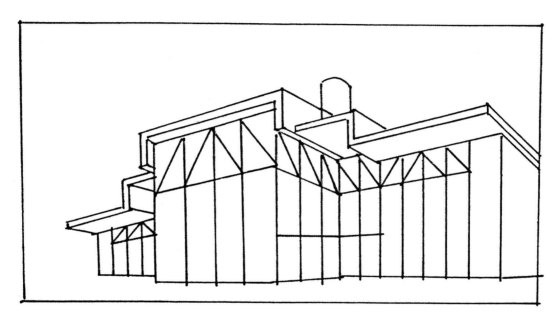

Solid and less penetrable at the front woodland entry, the structure conversely is visually open at the rear sliding screen wall on the lakeside.

Inside and outside space and forms all merge and come simultaneously into awareness.

outside of usual time and usual space

The qualities of the landscape and this place play out as if on a screen, while the inhabitant always remains at the center. Natural processes in the landscape are revealed, entropic and vital, on the dissolving boundaries between things, as time collapses into the continual present moment.

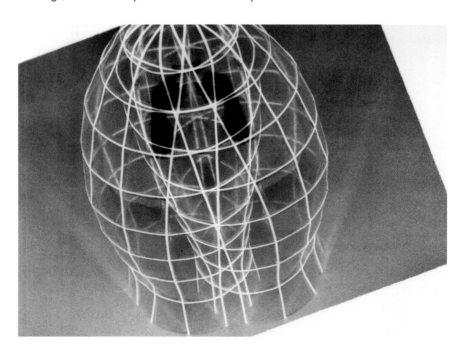

This project evolved as a bridge in many senses. Bridges connect opposite and disparate entities, and are structures that sit on boundaries, allowing transition from one point to the next.

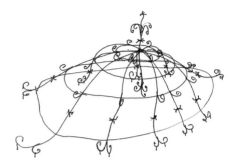

Seamed metal panels are detailed up and down the steps of the roof, like a piece of fabric. The panels are draped over all the horizontal and vertical roof surfaces, bridging left to right.

As a place of refuge, the project connects the land, with its daily concerns and preoccupations, to the water with its timeless, ephemeral, and contemplative quality. In a larger sense, the arched bridging structure might engender a connection between the material and the sublime.

in luminous support and reconciliation

What is inside and outside and what is beyond the structure can be seen all at once. In this way the structure reveals its nature and purpose clearly.

The interior canopy of the stepped ceiling can be sensed all at once, and the spaces are filled continually with light.

In sleep, sleep itself can become palpable like film on the surface of water, transparent, only a spindly effect without quite a full hold. Underneath this, things actually do happen, and we are always the same throughout.

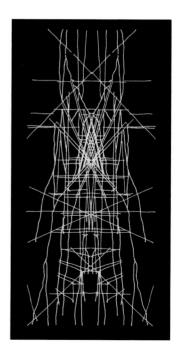

Toward the lake, a reinforced glass screen wall contains a triangulated structural bridge truss of variable size that allows maximum visibility and openness.

This thin truss structure, hidden within the window frames eliminates the need for the large supporting columns and beams that would normally be part of a roof canopy system.

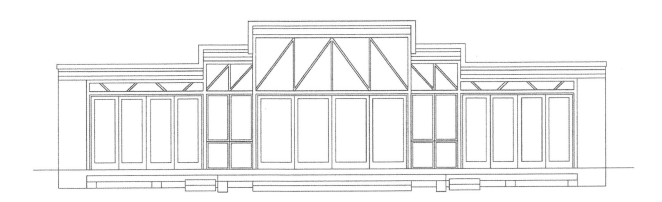

lifting up and floating, soaring

The bridging elements are simple and abstracted, warm and present, and in visual balance. In feeling they are also low scale and personal.

At the same time, reflections project a seeming landscape and their experience confronts.

Perception and time, form and space, all enfold
upon themselves.

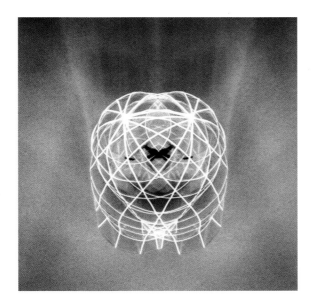

energized, fierce and gritty, gestating, molecular
and steadfast

There is a transparency to this house that allows
the visual bridging of land and water. All interior
spaces are loosely defined, and merge while
maintaining privacy where necessary. The use
of symmetry and frontally suggest body resemblance, and allow for a centered awareness.

This structure reveals rather than obscures.

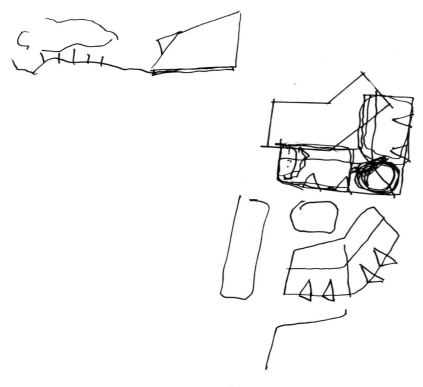

lakeside structures

within floating, hovering, flying, soaring scenes, dreams within dreams, vault-like, head-shaped spaces

into a world made strange

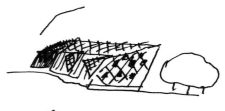

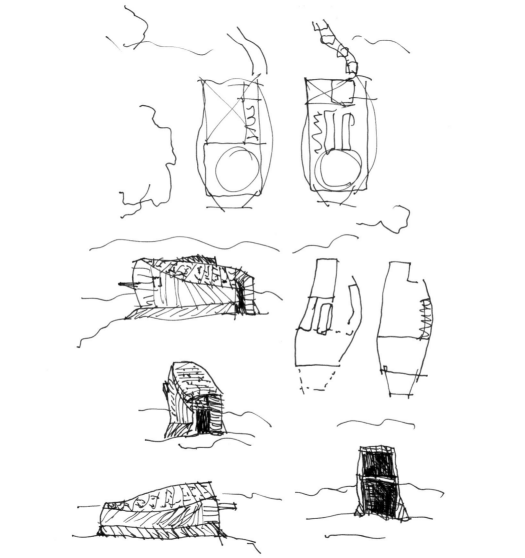

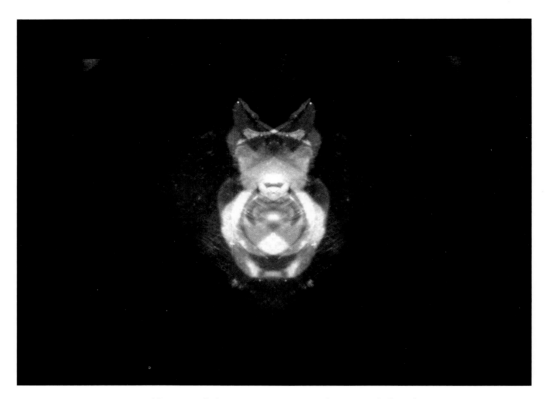

Dream-like or real, these spaces twist and turn into light. They resolve themselves or not. It is a contest involving the viewer and what is seen.

spinning around, spinning right, climbing up a hill, the sky half dark, half spiral-colored swirling light

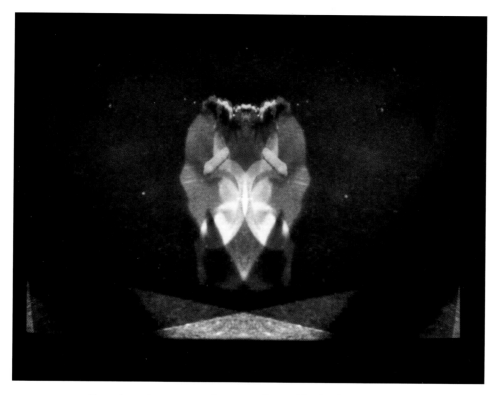

Step down into a room that is configured for both the arousal and the weakening of fear. A room that engenders reliance and determination.

Footstep-like sounds, clatter down, from the distant echoing corridor and chamber-like place.

At the perimeter the black slashes and cuts are
seen as voids in the earth, empty of content.
Dangerous and dark, they circumscribe the edge
of the dance.

black shadows and ghost forms, imperceptible,
un-documentable, a hole in what is

objects for a dance set and the pull
of dream-like reconfigurations

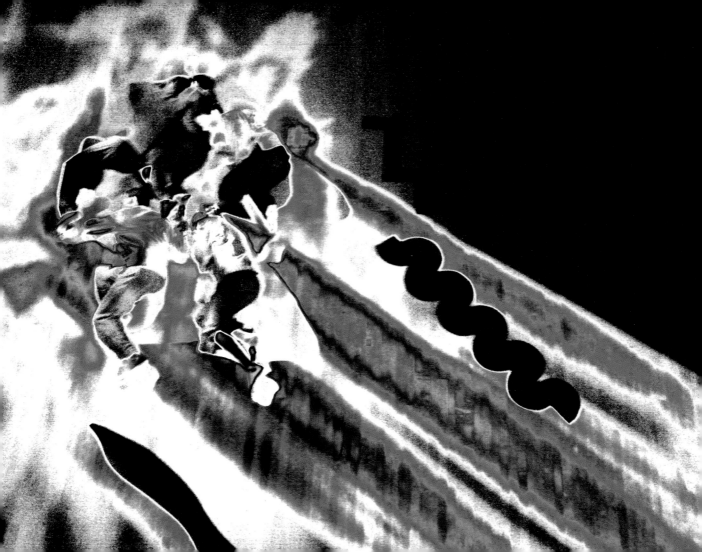

LEBBEUS WOODS
GORDON GILBERT: BEYOND THE EDGE

Among all the speculations about an electronic culture, about architecture that appears and disappears with the speed of shifting electrons and photons, therefore of light, about the constantly dissolving boundaries of thought and of being, about liquid architecture (so often spoken of today, but rarely visualized), about plasma architecture and fluid dynamics, Gordon Gilbert's architecture seems both prophetic and inevitable. After machines have suffered their ultimate entropy and can inform architecture no more, indeed, after mechanical patterns have lost their hold over human consciousness, it may be possible to conceive and construct an architecture of cybernetic dimensions and the ephemeral substance of thought. Gilbert's is an experimental architecture, evoking possibilities and invoking limits.

Gilbert's thought-experiments and structures are grown as much as built. They are not made of parts and fragments, welded together into a mosaic or collage, but are organic, synthetic and whole Architects today are still wedded too much to the idea of assemblage to have enthusiasm for holisms which produce organic unities. Disparities of construction reflect the modern and post-modern romance with fragmentation. Being a romantic of a different kind, Gilbert goes directly to the idea of architecture as integral with being. He tacitly assumes that the aim of technology is to become invisible, bestowing its powers with no presence of its own. Miniaturization is only a step towards complete integration. When the machine becomes invisible, its extension of human capacities - to see far, move fast, penetrate deeply - will be genetic. They will have become, in a word, fully human, and no longer prosthetic extensions. Then Gilbert's

pulsating and intricately woven houses will seem utterly natural forms of both body and mind.

A key to comprehending Gilbert's work is his use of symmetry. It is not a classical symmetry, which relies on a tripartite A-B-A schema, but the bilateral symmetry of common organisms, among which the human must be counted.

This path to formal order has been challenged in the Twentieth Century as being too limiting, too static in its energy. This is the age of plurality, of fragmentation and asymmetry, of diversity and complexity, of chaos theory and political anarchy, of the richness of possibilities and the disparity of results. The breaking of symmetry is all that astrophysicists can claim as the basis for the formation of galaxies, planets and their evolving forms of life. Even the human body is only approximately symmetrical. In light of this understanding, Gilbert's symmetries are disconcertingly perfect, portending finality, conclusion, and - in and organic sense - death. Leaving aside his subtle interweaving of asymmetrical effects, such as shadows or rays of light, one is left with an absolute mirroring of elements, an absolute equality of halves.

Is this a regression to anachronistic ideas of the Divine? Is Gilbert's architecture a slipping back into a kind of pre conscious, "when Man and Nature were one?" Or is it a premonition of advanced technological simplicity, of a time when all things will return to a primal directness, uncomplicated by mechanical breakdowns and computer viruses, the artifices of obsessive imbalance and its exciting but inherently neurotic interest? Gilbert's world stands before us in images he has made of landscapes and structures he claims for the domain of an absolute architecture, implicit for our desire for a primordial absolute, enticing us even as it warns.

His work is a critique of the idea of progress. At the same time it provokes us with the idea of perfectibility, which can only occur at the end of some sequence of calculated events, some conscious progression or progression of consciousness.

Obviously, his work is not without its ironies. Indeed, once encountered, they become central to it. Gilbert makes his designs for spaces and structures using the very machines they render obsolete, photocopiers, cameras, enlargers, all employed by anonymous technicians. By placing his drawings and holograms and model photographs in the hands of others, Gilbert consciously relinquishes some degree of control even though he continually fights to regain it.

While every architect does this, in Gilbert's case the result is critical, because his architecture only exists for now only in the resulting images. Even their publication in an architectural journal presents a crisis. Each transformation involves shifts in subtleties that cannot be reversed. What is "lost in the process" is forever lost. Whatever is "gained" can only be counted in terms of communions with an unknown Nature, whether in the guise of the human or not.

Gilbert's work raises the possibility of thinking of architecture in terms of states of being only dimly visible through the haze of electronic mass culture. These may be states of a recondite Sublime, as suggested in his texts, or a sublimation of the human itself, revealed as a dissolution of spatial and temporal experience in an ineffable Unity.

One of the less visible members of the Research Institute for Experimental Architecture, Gordon Gilbert is a registered architect, who worked independently for many years, quietly producing his projects, publishing and showing only rarely. His strange and unsettling structures exist beyond the outer edge of what is presently known or, perhaps, desired to be known. They appear as monuments to human aspiration, and. in their visual evocation, as instruments of a difficult, but not utterly remote transcendence.

Lebbeus Woods (1940-2012) was one of the most prominent architectural visionaries, whose experimental works have been exhibited worldwide. Published work includes *OneFiveFour, War and Architecture, Radical Reconstruction, The Storm and the Fall,* and *Slow Manifesto: Lebbeus Woods Blog.* He was Professor of Architecture at The Cooper Union in New York City.

This essay first appeared in "A + U: Architecture and Urbanism" (number 93-07) and is reproduced here with permission of the Estate of Lebbeus Woods.

ZVI HECKER
WRITING

The significance and uniqueness of hand drawings lies not in the clarity of their message, but in their inherent imperfection.

As our mind is never in complete control of our hand, it is free to create signs, left open for interpretation. Not once was I surprised at how hand drawing can evoke possibilities that most probably I would not have been able to imagine conciously.

No successful solution can be reached by sequential analysis but rather by intuitive synthesis. In this respect, hand drawings help to channel the vague ponderings of the mind into visual images of a germinating concept.

Architecture is above all an act of magic; not because a magician is at work, but rather because it hides more than it reveals. What we look at, what we see, is only a reflected image of what we cannot see: the architecture's soul. Invisible and immaterial, it displays a surprising degree of resistance to the passing of time and ever changing fashion.

I believe that only beauty endures. Beauty is the final destination of the artist's work. No map will indicate its precise location. One has to build one's own means of transport to get there.

Hand drawing is such a vehicle for me.

Needless to say I have great sympathy with your thinking, building ...

Born in Cracow, Poland, Zvi Hecker subsequently grew up in Samarkand, Uzbekistan. He studied architecture at the Technion in Haifa, Israel and painting at the Avni Institute of Art and Design in Tel Aviv, where he set up his first architectural practice. He has taught at the Universite Laval in Quebec City, and the University of Applied Arts in Vienna. In 1991, he set up his architectural practice in Berlin. His recent book titled *Sketches* is published by Hatje Cantz.

MICHAEL SORKIN
FOR GORDON

Gordon and I know each other through Leb Woods, a
friend and spirit guide to us both. Leb was not simply
a design genius but an ethical exemplar and one of
architecture's priests. That is, he believed in architecture's artistic sacrality, its capacity to embody ideas, and
in its autonomy. This led him to the position – not unique
among visionaries – that architecture always confronted
the risk of dissipation when it was contaminated by the
quotidian. Leb was a Platonist in his anxiety about the
spaces of becoming, about the contingency of the meaning of building. One of the things that attracted him to
zones of conflict – Sarajevo, divided Berlin, the DMZ
– was that architecture was tested there, that its literal
integrity was continuously violated, creating a special
condition of meaning and a space of testing, a margin.
The same questing distinguished his extra-gravitational
work, architectures that had passed over the limits of
buildings most fundamental constraint: gravity.

One of crises that Leb's style of speculation skirted was
construction. Throughout his career, Leb danced at this
periphery, refusing to yield the belief that translation
always put meaning at risk. He did not make buildings
in the conventional sense – although what he drew was
surely often constructable – but he did increasingly move
into interventions that worked in all three dimensions,
what might be called "installations" in the art world.
There were often very abstract, spatializations of drawing or instruments to measure both the palpabilities and
the character of space, which he saw as something very
much alive, aswim with charges and ineffable particles
that he sought to capture and reveal. He took us all into
a reality that was not an alternative but a distillation, a

place of intense ambiguity that encourage the search for many paths.

After not seeing Gordon for a number of years I was both pleased to hear from him and especially happy that he reintroduced himself via that old problematic of drawing vs. building, a question at the heart of many conversations we'd had more than two decades earlier when we were both part of Leb's Research Institute for Experimental Architecture. This book is full of drawings from that time, "abstract" depictions of "pure" architectonic issues, including bilateralism, representation, the quality of line, collage, and other diffusions of meaning, work still full of mystery and charge that probes architecture at its edges.

What is added now are a series of built projects that are fully congruent in spirit with his earlier investigations into realms for which the exigencies of construction are not an issue. Which begs the question of how an architect prepares to cross over, the nature of the study, the character of the seam between what appears immaterial and the transformation of the embodied ideas into something very concrete.

Gordon's chosen metaphor is transparency and it's a good one, recalling his own investigations into permeability and reflecting Robert Slutzky's parsing of the quality into the literal and the phenomenal. Both ways, it's an obvious focus of Gordon's architectural taste, with its preference for a clarity of construction and detail and a spatial movement between in and out that's carefully modulated to maximize exposure in the contexts of sun, view, privacy, and personality.

The buildings in this book have supple differences in their geometry, materiality, mood, and chosen ambiguities. All have a clear sense of place and purpose, which implies a collection of singularities within the framework of a consistent sensibility. Evoking both his own favored images – a Siamese temple, a Chinese junk, a jungle, a bridge, a lake – these buildings explore the relations between what is fixed and what ephemeral as the mood of the dweller combines with the rhythms of shifting nature encountered through the elusive membrane of transparent glass and ideas.

Michael Sorkin is Principal of the Michael Sorkin Studio, a global architectural and urbanist practice, President and founder of Terreform, a non-profit institute researching the forms and methods of just and sustainable urbanism, Distinguished Professor of Architecture and Director of the Graduate Program in Urban Design at The City College of New York, and architecture critic for *The Nation*.

CHRISTIAN W. THOMSEN
DREAM DANCER'S ARCHITECTURAL CHOREOGRAPHIES

> "The heart not the head must be the guide"
> Arthur Erickson

Inge, my wife, loves kaleidoscopes. From early childhood on she has been fascinated by the interplay of little colored pieces of glass with mirrors and reflections, by the patterns and symmetries created by just rotating the cardboard tube, by the beautiful images produced which work on your imagination. In 1945/46 when she was very young and living together with her mother as a refugee from bombed out Stuttgart in a little Swabian village, her father far away in a British PoW camp, her kaleidoscope was one of her few dearly loved possessions.

Yet there was something else, that incessant curiosity and Faustian drive, to know what was really inside, to know how the construction worked, to see those precious stones one by one, to hold them in her hand. Finally the four-year-old girl managed to open her kaleidoscope. And all of a sudden the charm, the magic, the beauty, the dreams had gone, she had destroyed them herself and she cried bitterly.

Almost sixty-seven years later Inge still keeps kaleidoscopes and is delighted by their changing symmetries and colorful beauty.

Some of Gordon Gilbert's drawings in his projects Subtle Architecture and Architecture of the Night resemble kaleidoscopic structures. What catches his attention are their crystalline structures and symmetries, their reflections and refractions on their way to the center, the core of which is impenetrable silence, the mystic, quasi-religious dissolving of self in a union of nature and man's longing for transcendence.

Gordon Gilbert also is a dancer, a dreamer, a visionary dream dancer, of dreams within dreams. As such his drawings are full of upward movement and change, rotating from rectangular structures into multifaceted round bodies with ever new sights and views.

Since Joseph Paxton's Crystal Palace (1851) the idea of transparent architecture has been connected with glass architecture. After all those 19th century exhibition halls, train stations, greenhouses and passages, theoretically glass architecture reached an early peak with the ideas, letters, drawings of the members of the so-called Crystal Chain (Gläserne Kette), Bruno Taut, Wenzel Hablik, the early Hans Scharoun, Hermann Finsterlin, Paul Scheerbart (being the most active members), exactly a century ago.

The interrelations between body and soul, between the material, the physical, and the spiritual form the central part of Bruno Taut's contributions to Crystal Chain. Just as the body could become spiritualized by transfiguration, in reverse the soul and spirit could take on architectural form through architecture as a medium. Taut believed that the perfect interpenetration of human faith and God's spirit would create the new Kingdom of Heaven. [1]

The idea of glass architecture combined with that American Dream of New Canaan, America as God's own chosen country was perfectly executed by Philip Johnson's Glass House New Canaan in 1949. Otherwise, in a spiritual way, Taut's thoughts come rather close to Gordon Gilbert's ideas. The latter connects them in his drawings with dance. And dance, without doubt, frequently has spiritual, even religious and mystic as well as mythic roots which in some cases are even connected with architecture.

The word *labyrinthos* derives from pre-Greek Minoan culture in ancient Crete, and in Homer's description it shows the complicated labyrinthian movements of a group of ritual dancers within a building also called Labyrinth. Secularized it became the term for a distinct and admirable stone building.

In the original concept of "Labyrinth," literary, visual, and ritual dance traditions merge with those of an architectural object. [2] Dance performs figurative movements in space comparable to architectural drawings, thereby ritually taking possession of that space. In modern times, the Argentinian tango, with all its sensual, erotic and ritual implications, is perhaps one of the best examples of that method.

In Gordon Gilbert's projects for this book, the two Florida houses come closest to a concept of architecture as dance. And as far as transparency is concerned, it is more an interior transparency in the Miesian sense of floating rooms and spaces, moving and merging dance-like, than that of an inside-out, outside-in transparent glass building.

Then Mies van der Rohe published his designs for a glass high-rise building in 1921 and thus, together with the floating room concept of his Barcelona Pavilion (1929), influenced modern architecture in a decisive way. After World War II, steel and glass constructions, together with curtain wall facades, became the constitutive element of high-rise and office buildings of the "International Style" from the 1950s to the 1970s.

In 1989 I was asked by a Munich based architectural magazine to write an article about those twelve architects living in Mies' famous Chicago Lake Shore Drive Apartment Buildings. Each of them had staged his particular apartment in a very personal, individual way, but always in accordance with Miesian ideas. Some of them invited me to their places when the evening crept in and one by one the lights in the surrounding high-rises went on. *Transparent Architecture* as Architecture of the Night: You need no excursions into the realm of theory to understand what is meant by such a concept, the experience just fills body and soul.

Transparency in a positive sense, inside-out, outside-in, open floating spaces, embedded in landscape structures and in nature, widening your living experience in a multi-sensorial way, was taken for granted with many low-rise buildings and single-unit houses. In California, I had the pleasure of seeing some of Richard Neutra's houses built in this way.

There are two of Gordon Gilbert's houses which evoke some of my most cherished remembrances as far as architecture is concerned and in which I certainly could imagine living for a certain time, Lake House and Bridge House. They remind me of some of Arthur Erickson's early houses: in particular Graham House (1962) and Smith House (1965), both in West Vancouver. Not in a way that suggests Gordon's Houses were imitations, but they breathe the same kind of spirit.

In the 1980s Arthur Erickson, very likely Canada's most eminent architect yet, became one of my best friends and most influential teachers ever. He took the untrained German professor of English and American Literature by the hand and taught him how to see, feel, experience, and understand architecture. His voice still rings in my ears as I hear him saying: "Christian, space has always been the spiritual dimension of architecture. It is not the physical statement of the structure so much as what it contains that moves us."

When Gordon Gilbert states of his Lake House that it "fans, folds and shifts," that his "spaces allow the senses to expand as the interior and exterior merge," the two architects prove to be spiritual brothers. What also relates them to each other is the bridge function and symbolism frequently met in their projects. The use of natural materials is another. Arthur's biggest use is Lethbridge University which spans over coulée-broken prairie landscapes in south-central Alberta.

One difference may be found in Gilbert's greater desire to finally dissolve all physicality in a kind of quasi-religious, mystic condensation of multisensory experiences. The comparisons also may not hold for Erickson's later

phases when he turned to major projects in glass, concrete and steel, but until his very end in 2009 they are valid with regard to the spiritual dimension of architecture.

I would like to spend time in all of Gordon's houses, just for the experience; not only because of their shifting viewpoints, but to feel how body and soul come to rest, enjoying nature near lake and woods. Moreover, I would like to see whether his intellectual and spiritual dances are physically comprehensible.

Our kids were lastingly influenced and shaped in their characters by having had the chance to often play in and around painter friend Gordon Smith's house while we lived in Vancouver: the Pacific Ocean ahead, sea eagles above, and the occasional bear in the neighborhood. But who can afford this kind of life? Only people with expansive parkland grounds? Middle class people often could and still can. In 1964 Gordon Smith's home cost CAD $ 65,000. I wouldn't even dare a guess at how much it is worth today.

Gordon Gilbert's Lake House of 2010 is, of course, much more modern, with its "reed-like bridging of hybrid members hidden within the window frames." I applaud him for that and also that there are corners and possible hiding places within.

In 1981 Viennese painter and singer-songwriter Arik Brauer had a song in the Austrian charts, the translation of which would run like this:

They have a house built,
They have us a house built,
They have us a house built here.
If rooms have only straight corners
Where should the dachshund hide?
Has the kitchen just an upright wall,
The butter goes rancid and the milk runs sour.

It just means that everybody's inner "dachshund" needs a place to hide, some privacy to rest unobserved, to recharge their batteries, to think, to dream, to make love.

Imagine all this in Philip Johnson's New Canaan or in his contemporary glass enthusiast's world famous architect-engineer Werner Sobek's hillside house in Stuttgart. Sobek, successor to Frei Otto as director of the Institute for Light Buildings, Design, and Construction at Stuttgart University holds his chair in Stuttgart as well as the Mies van der Rohe professorship at the Illinois Institute of Technology in Chicago.

Sobek's Stuttgart Glasshouse, a high tech Zero Energy House (2002), soon became world famous. But what does it mean to live there, even if there are no curious neighbors to spy on you? His son couldn't stand it and moved into the garage.

In contrast to that, Gilbert's ideas of transparency, realized in the projects of this book, look thoroughly enjoyable. But when it comes to high scale glass facades and glass buildings there is an obvious clash between dreams, ideas, and reality.

Transparent architecture fell into disrepute with the pseudo-transparent glass palaces of banks, insurance companies, and office buildings, which allow the inside-out view but are opaque from outside in, just like their business practices. There the idea of transparency in architecture has been perverted into the reverse. The absolute climax in hypocritical pseudo-transparency is reached in the Fort Meade Center buildings of the NSA, two enormous glass cubes.

For years we have been dimly aware in Europe that each of our transatlantic phone calls, emails ,and other internet connections might be hooked, caught, and stored by one or the other of those countless American Secret Services that disregard sovereignty, international laws and their own constitution.

Now we know for sure that the idea behind the world's largest super computer under construction, the two billion dollar NSA PRISM Project in Utah, is the total transparency of all mankind. Apart from internet connections and what is already being done, my friends in our Institute of High and Highest Frequency tell me that in the near future it will be technically possible to have cameras and scanners which not only show your house from a great distance, but also allow others to look into it, even into the persons moving inside. You sit in your bathtub and Big Brother NSA is looking into your stomach, seeing what you have eaten for dinner! In an unholy alliance with British Secret Services they want to become omnipotent. The state with its computers playing God-father who punishes and rewards.

The end of such a system will be its breakdown by total data overkill. We have experienced this with East Germany, the former communist so-called German Democratic Republic (GDR), which broke down in 1989 not only because of its rotten industry, but also because they had ineffectively hired one tenth of the population as agents and informal collaborators of their State Security Service (Stasi). Eventually this led to an uncontrollable mass of useless data and the system collapsed.

Total transparency? Gordon Gilbert confronts us with such a project, too. A series of glass cubes, erected in front of a skyline (New York), surrounded by water. It could be a floating, crystalline exhibition showcase, it would be a splendid, light-emitting landmark seen from the sea. But seen from the land it would be more difficult.

It shows characteristics of a temple or other religious building of worship, with a Holy Grail or shrine in the center. Architectural cubes have a long tradition, from the Kaaba (cube) in Mecca, the holiest of all places of worship in Islam, to the present series of museum cubes erected in numerous German cities.

Winnipeg architect Etienne Gaboury once took me on a walk round his Royal Canadian Mint, a crystalline glass building, like a diamond reflecting itself in a surrounding lake. Spiraling your way around the building you could watch the production of coins for currencies from fifty countries.

Moshe Safdie took me on tours through his National Gallery of Canada (1983-1989) in Ottawa while still under construction and after its completion. Crystal towers form its central image and give the building its special flair.

Once I attended a service at Philip Johnson's LA-Garden Grove Community Church (1976-1980), a Hollywood-Opera like experience. Reflecting pools or ponds are always part of the scenery, transparency or kaleidoscope refractions, as mentioned at the beginning of my essay, are always part of the show, symbols of purity, of life, of beauty, of preciousness.

Gordon Gilbert takes his model from the far distant past, the Babylonian ziggurat, mountain of the gods, terraced Temple Towers, forerunners of the Tower of Babylon. That of Sialk in Mesopotamia, now hidden deep in Iran, comes closest to his design.

To quote Gordon: "The translucent, semi-transparent, stepped, crystalline structure completes itself visually in the reflecting pool. Its wholeness is comprised of actual and reflected imagery, and the form is completed in the viewer's own mind. Thus the seeming solidity of the structure is in great part illusory."

That is the old game of perception. Illusion or reality, what is imagination, what legend and old lore? Central questions of every religion. They all claim to be in possession of absolute truths. And in the center of Gordon's design there is a kind of undefined structure, shrine, Holy Grail.
I appreciate the built projects, Gordon Gilbert's houses. I would like to see them in reality, spend some time there.

And I am all in with the dancers in his dream influenced set designs for a New York City dance company. In 1961 Perry Como wrote his song "Dream on little dreamer, dream on." Is Gordon only a little dreamer? In a recent email he wrote to me: "Life is quite varied and inspiring, don't you agree? It can be joy..." I look at the photo of the man I haven't seen for twenty three years. We are of the same generation. Before I took to the production of documentary films I used to direct plays, once or twice a year. Some lines from one of the texts I most admire come to my mind, Prospero's farewell speech in Shakespeare's farewell play *The Tempest*. Those lines are among the best ever written, and they even have something to do with architecture:

You do look, my son, in a moved sort,
As if you were dismay'd: be cheerful, sir.
Our revels now are ended. These our actors,
As I foretold you, were all spirits and
Are melted into air, into thin air:
And, like the baseless fabric of this vision,
The cloud-capp'd towers, the gorgeous palaces,
The solemn temples, the great globe itself,
Ye all which it inherit, shall dissolve
And, like this insubstantial pageant faded,
Leave not a rack behind. We are such stuff
As dreams are made on, and our little life
Is rounded with a sleep...

Gordon would make a good Prospero. Yet, the guy looks so optimistic!

Christian W. Thomsen was born in Dresden, and is one of Germany's most prolific writers on literature, art, culture, and architecture. He became professor and founding senator of the Department of English at the University of Siegen. Many of his books have developed into international classics, including *Literature: Maneaters in Literature and Art* and *Experimental Architects*. Also finding wide acclaim are *Visionary Architecture* and *The Art of Erotic Building*. He has been visiting professor at UBC, UCLA, and at the Bartlett School of Architecture in London.

[1] Ian Boyd Whyte, ed., *Crystal Chain Letters: Architectural Fantasies by Bruno Taut and his Circle*, MIT Press 1985, p. 7
[2] Hermann Kern, *Labyrinthe: Erscheinungen und Deutungen: 5000 Jahre Gegenwart eines Urbildes*, München, 1982, p. 18-19

GORDON GILBERT
SELECTED PUBLICATIONS

"Lake House." Archipendium 2016. Berlin: Archimap Publishers, 2016, 22.

"RIEA: The Backstory." Slow Manifesto: Lebbeus Woods Blog. NY: Princeton Architectural Press, 2015, 184-186.

"Wooden Architecture." Revija HISE. #83. Ljubljana, Slovenia, March 2014, 60-61.

Thomsen, Christian, "Dream Dancer's Architectural Choreographies. Remarks on Gordon Gilbert's book Transparent Architecture." Siegen, Germany, 2013.

Jodidio, Philip, editor, "Gordon Gilbert." Wood Architecture Now 2. Cologne, Germany: Taschen Publications. Published in English and German, 2013, 140-53.

"Bridge House." Wood Design & Building. Number 57. Ottawa: Dovetail, 2012, 16-18.

"Lake House." Wood Design & Building. Number 52. Ottawa: Dovetail, 2011, 10-12.

"Split House." Building through Time. Miami: University of Miami Press, 2002, 33-34.

Gilbert, Gordon, "Architecture of the Night." projects in A+U - Architecture and Urbanism. Tokyo, Japan: A+U Publishing Company Ltd, 93-07, 3-19.

Woods, Lebbeus, "Gordon Gilbert: Beyond the Edge." A+U - Architecture and Urbanism. Critical project essay. Tokyo, Japan: A+U Publishing Company Ltd, 93-07, 20-21.

"Berlin Exposition of Experimental Architecture." Article in A+U - Architecture and Urbanism. Tokyo, Japan: A+U Publishing Company Ltd, 90:10, 30-43.

"Experimentelle Architektur in der Gallerie Aedes." Metropol Gesellschaft. Berlin: 15.03.90.

Gilbert, Gordon, "Subtle Architecture." RIEA: The First Conference Publication. NY: Princeton Architectural Press, and Berlin, Germany: Aedes Gallerie, 16-21.

Woods, Lebbeus, "Experimental Architecture: A Commentary." Journal of Theory and Criticism in Architecture and the Arts 2. Denver: University of Colorado Press, 12-13.

"Storefront Exhibition Newsprints." Documentation for several exhibitions including "Existence," and "Future of Storefront." NY: Storefront for Art and Architecture Books.

GORDON GILBERT was born in Washington DC, and raised in Latin America. He graduated from the University of Miami with degrees in Architecture and in Art History, and established his own architectural office, Gordon Gilbert Architect, in New York City in 1984. He was a founding member of the Research Institute for Experimental Architecture, and exhibited his work in its First Conference Exhibition in Berlin.

He has also developed conceptual and experimental drawings over the years including drawings for the project 'Architecture of the Night', exhibited internationally and published in the journal *A+U: Architecture and Urbanism*. He is a past fellow in Architecture at the New York Foundation for the Arts (NYFA) and at the MacDowell Colony in Peterborough, New Hampshire. The office has designed sets and portable objects for productions by New York City dance companies, and has completed numerous design and construction projects nationwide.

All conceptual drawings and models throughout the book are from the project 'Subtle Architecture and the Subtle Body' and from the project 'Architecture of the Night.'

Other built works in order of appearance include:

Split House and Studio, in a tropical hammock, Miami, Florida
Stilt House, using hurricane construction, Coconut Grove, Florida
Lake House, on Echo Lake, in the Catskill Region of New York
Crystalline Glass Memorial proposal for New York City
Bridge House, on Echo Lake, in the Catskill Region of New York
Set Designs for Zendora Dance Company, New York City

ORO EDITIONS
Publishers of Architecture, Art, and Design
Gordon Goff: Publisher
www.oroeditions.com
info@oroeditions.com

Lake House photography: David Sundberg/Esto: Cover, pages 38, 41, 43, 44, 46, 47, 51, 52, 54, 55, 57.
Bridge House photography: David Sundberg/Esto: pages 71, 73, 74, 77, 78, 79, 81, 82, 83, 85.
Zendora Dance Company photography: Miana Jun: pages 92, 93.

Edited by: Gordon Gilbert
Book Design: Matthew Ricke
Color Separations and Printing: ORO Group Ltd.
Printed in China.

With appreciation to the contributors of the essays in this book, Michael Sorkin, Zvi Hecker, Lebbeus Woods, and Christian W. Thomsen, and to Judith Meyerowitz, Arne Leland, ALC Construction, Pratts Real Estate, Jay Zeiger, Val Carroll, Consolidated Construction, William Maguire, Deborah Hecht, Ed Laurion, Dana Hoff, Perspective Arts, Don Dietsche, Nancy Zendora, David Sundberg, Aleksandra Wagner, Erica Stoller/Esto, and to Gordon Goff, Jake Anderson, and Matthew Ricke of ORO Editions.

By working with GLOBAL ReLeaf, ORO Editions makes a continuous effort to minimize the overall carbon footprint of its publications, arranging to plant trees to replace those used in the manufacturing of its books. An international campaign run by American Forests, Global ReLeaf is one of the world's oldest nonprofit conservation organizations.

TRANSPARENT

ARCHITECTURE